D0710371

★ *GREAT SPORTS TEAMS* ★

THE SAN FRANCISCO

GIANTS

BASEBALL TEAM

David Pietrusza

Enslow Publishers, Inc.

40 Industrial Road   PO Box 38
Box 398   Aldershot
Berkeley Heights, NJ 07922   Hants GU12 6BP
USA   UK

http://www.enslow.com

To Giants fan David Walsh

Library of Congress Cataloging-in-Publication Data

Pietrusza, David, 1949–
        The San Francisco Giants baseball team / David Pietrusza.
            p. cm. — (Great sports teams)
        Includes bibliographical references and index.
        Summary: Examines the history of the Giants baseball team including their
early days in New York, their move to San Francisco, and their successes in
the early 1990s.
        ISBN 0-7660-1284-0
        1. San Francisco Giants (Baseball team)—History Juvenile literature. [1. San
Francisco Giants (Baseball team)—History. 2. Baseball—History.] I. Title.
II. Series.
GV875.S35P54   2000
96.357'64'0979461—dc21   99-30157
                                                                                    CIP

Printed in the United States of America

10 9 8 7 6 5 4 3 2 1

To Our Readers: All Internet addresses in this book were active and appropriate
when we went to press. Any comments or suggestions can be sent by e-mail to
Comments@enslow.com or to the address on the back cover.

Illustration Credits: AP/Wide World Photos.

Cover Illustration: AP/Wide World Photos.

Cover Description: Giants outfielder Barry Bonds

CONTENTS

1 "The Giants Win the Pennant"....... 5

2 New York, New York............... 11

3 Giant Immortals 17

4 Giants Managers................. 23

5 The City by the Bay 29

6 Ups and Downs.................. 35

Statistics 40

Chapter Notes................... 43

Glossary........................ 44

Further Reading 46

Index 47

Where to Write 48

*S*ome baseball fans consider Willie Mays to be the best all-around player in baseball history.

"THE GIANTS WIN THE PENNANT"

I n New York City, Giants fans had always hated the Brooklyn Dodgers, and Dodgers fans had always hated the New York Giants.

Inner-City Rivalry

Now it was 1951. The Dodgers—featuring such Hall of Famers as second baseman Jackie Robinson, center fielder Duke Snider, shortstop Pee Wee Reese, and catcher Roy Campanella—had shot out in front of the Giants. On August 11, Brooklyn held a 13 1/2 game lead over New York. It looked as if the Dodgers would easily take the National League pennant.

But the Giants had their own stars—center fielder Willie Mays, third baseman Monte Irvin, shortstop Alvin Dark, left fielder Bobby Thomson, and starting pitchers Sal Maglie and Larry Jansen—and they were not about to give up. Giants manager Leo Durocher, who had formerly managed Brooklyn, drove his players on as they steadily narrowed the gap between themselves and their rivals. At one point the Giants won sixteen straight games, and when the season ended the teams were tied for first.

_____

The Fight for the Pennant

Now, Brooklyn and New York would face each other in a three-game playoff to decide the National League pennant. The Giants won the first game 3–1 as Bobby Thomson and Monte Irvin homered off Dodgers right-hander Ralph Branca. Brooklyn evened the series in Game 2, humiliating New York by a 10–0 score.

It would all depend on Game 3. The score remained knotted at 1–1 after seven innings. Then the Dodgers burst through, scoring three runs in the top of the eighth inning. The Giants went down in order in the bottom of the inning. Giants pitcher Larry Jansen came in from the bullpen, and held the Dodgers scoreless in the top of the ninth. The Giants were down to their last three outs.

"Fellows," Durocher told his players, "you've done just a hell of a job all year long. I'm proud of every one of you. We've got three whacks at them, boys! It's not over yet. Let's go out there and give them all we got, and let's leave this ball field, win or lose, with our heads in the air."[1]

Alvin Dark led off with a single to right. For some reason (even though Dark's run was meaningless) Dodgers first baseman Gil Hodges held Dark on first, leaving a big hole on the right side of the infield. Giants right fielder Don Mueller took advantage of the situation and singled past Hodges, sending Dark to

*B*obby Thomson came up in the bottom of the ninth inning. He hit a long drive down the left-field line. The flight of the ball is shown by the dotted line.

third. Dodgers starter Don Newcombe then settled down and got Irvin to pop up to Hodges. Up came first baseman Whitey Lockman, who ripped a double to left, scoring Dark and sending Mueller to third. Mueller hurt his ankle on the play, and Leo Durocher sent catcher Clint Hartung in to pinch-run for him.

The Starter is Taken Out

Dodgers manager Chuck Dressen decided it was time to take Newcombe out of the game. He brought in Ralph Branca.

The first batter Branca would face was Bobby Thomson, who had homered off him in Game 1. "Before I settled in to bat," Thomson later remembered, "Leo said to me, 'Bobby, if you ever hit one, hit one now.' I didn't say anything, but in my mind I was thinking base hit, not homer."[2]

Thomson was not only thinking base hit, he was thinking too much. He watched as Branca laid a curve right down the middle. It was a pitch he should have hit easily, but he never moved his bat. No one was angrier with Thomson than he was with himself.

Now came Branca's second pitch. It was, thought Thomson, "a bad ball, high and inside."[3] This time, Thomson swung. The ball headed toward the left-field wall. It looked like it would carom off the wall, scoring Hartung and maybe Lockman. If Lockman scored, the game would be tied.

The Long Drive

But it was not off the wall. "There's a long drive!" screamed Giants radio broadcaster Russ Hodges. "It's going to be, I believe [a home run]! The Giants win the pennant! The Giants win the pennant! The Giants win the pennant! The Giants win the pennant! Bobby Thomson hits into the lower deck of the left-field stands! The Giants win the pennant!"[4]

Leo Durocher, Bobby Thomson, and the New York Giants had staged the most dramatic comeback in their history—maybe in *all* of baseball history.

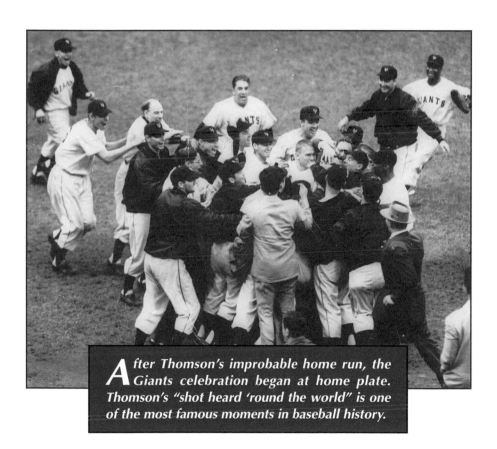

*A*fter Thomson's improbable home run, the Giants celebration began at home plate. Thomson's "shot heard 'round the world" is one of the most famous moments in baseball history.

*C*hristy Mathewson shows off the pitching motion that won him 373 games. When the Hall of Fame inducted its first class in 1936, Mathewson was one of the first players enshrined.

NEW YORK, NEW YORK

The New York Giants started back in 1883, after the old Troy, New York, National League franchise folded. The remnants of the team moved to New York City, where manager Jim Mutrie dubbed them his "Giants"—and the name stuck.

Early Success

The Giants won pennants in 1888 and 1889, but in the 1890s owner Andrew Freedman frequently changed Giants players and managers. The result was chaos—and bad teams. That all changed in 1902 when John McGraw arrived from Baltimore to manage the team. McGraw brought with him a nucleus of fine players from Baltimore, including two Hall of Famers, catcher Roger Bresnahan, and pitcher Joe "Iron Man" McGinnity. He also developed a young pitcher already on the Giants roster, Christy Mathewson, also known as the Big Six. Mathewson would soon turn into the finest pitcher of his era. "To me," said John McGraw, "he was pretty much the perfect type of pitching machine. He had the stature and strength, and he had tremendous speed. There never was another pitcher like Mathewson."[1]

By 1904, McGraw's Giants had won their first pennant—but stubbornly refused to play the Boston Red Sox, champions of the newly established American League, in the World Series. The following season, 1905, Mathewson won 31 games as the Giants captured another pennant. This time the Giants took part in the World Series. The Big Six shut out the Philadelphia A's three times, and the Giants became world champions.

In 1908, the Giants lost the pennant to the Chicago Cubs on first baseman Fred Merkle's famous base running bonehead play. Merkle failed to touch second base, and cost New York a crucial victory.

New York bounced back to win pennants in 1911, 1912, 1913, and 1917, although they lost the World Series each year. In the 1912 World Series, they suffered another heartbreaker, as New York center fielder Fred Snodgrass muffed an easy fly ball in the 10th inning of Game 7.

A New Group of Stars

Christy Mathewson was gone by 1920, but McGraw had such Hall of Famers in his lineup as second baseman Frankie Frisch, first baseman George Kelly, third baseman Fred Lindstrom, shortstop Travis "Stonewall"

Jackson, and outfielder Ross "Pep" Youngs. The club ran off a streak of four straight pennants from 1921 through 1924, beating Babe Ruth and the Yankees in the World Series in both 1921 and 1922.

In 1932, hard-hitting first baseman Bill Terry replaced McGraw as Giants manager. In 1933, 1936, and 1937 the Giants again won pennants. Terry (who hit .401 in 1930, and through 1999 is the last National Leaguer to crack the .400 barrier), outfielder Mel Ott (511 lifetime homers), and screw-balling southpaw "King Carl" Hubbell (253 career wins, 154 losses) were

Over the 1936–37 seasons, Carl Hubbell won 24 straight games for the Giants.

*G*iants manager Leo Durocher led his team from 13 1/2 games behind, to tie the Dodgers and force a one-game playoff to decide the 1951 National League pennant.

the Giants' big stars of the 1930s. Ott replaced Terry as manager in 1942, and lasted until 1948, but he never won a pennant.

Durocher's Team

Leo Durocher then took over. He transformed a slugging—but losing—team into a hustling, scrappy, winning team. Durocher's stars included second baseman Eddie "The Brat" Stanky, shortstop Alvin Dark, left fielder Bobby Thomson, third baseman Monte Irvin (a former Negro Leagues star), and exciting center fielder Willie "Say Hey" Mays. "There was a period when he could have been Most Valuable Player eight or nine years in a row," Irvin once said of Mays. "He was that valuable to the club."[2]

In 1951, the Giants caught the Dodgers and forced the exciting three-game playoff series for the pennant. In 1954, the Giants again won the pennant. This time they faced the Cleveland Indians in the World Series. The Indians had won a then-American-League-record 111 games in the regular season. The Giants surprised the Indians—and the baseball world—by sweeping Cleveland in four straight games.

The Giants Head West

But that was the New York Giants' last hurrah. Attendance was down. In 1957, both the Giants and their longtime rivals, the Brooklyn Dodgers, moved to California. The Dodgers relocated to Los Angeles; the Giants moved to San Francisco. A new era was about to begin.

*M*el Ott generated power by lifting his front foot before he swung the bat. He could also hit for average, though, finishing with a career mark of .304.

GIANT IMMORTALS

The Giants have boasted many fine players in their long history. The following players either already have been elected to Baseball's Hall of Fame—or, in the case of Barry Bonds—will be:

Christy Mathewson

Christy Mathewson was certainly a great pitcher—he's the coholder of the National League (NL) record for career victories, with 373 wins, and he holds the modern NL record with 37 wins in one season. But he was much more than that. He was a tremendous role model for the youth of the generation that followed 1900. Mathewson was well educated, and always a gentleman.

"Mathewson was the greatest pitcher who ever lived," marveled longtime Philadelphia A's manager Connie Mack. "He had knowledge, judgment, perfect control and form. It was wonderful to watch him pitch when he wasn't pitching against you."[1]

Bill Terry

Giants first baseman Bill Terry was the last National League batter to hit .400 in the 1900s. He did it in 1930 when he batted .401, but that one year was no fluke. From 1923 to 1936 he batted a solid .341. When John McGraw retired in 1932, Terry became Giants manager and led them to pennants in 1933 (when the Giants beat the Senators in the World Series), 1936, and 1937. He was elected to the Hall of Fame in 1954.

Mel Ott

Bill Terry hit for average, but little Mel Ott hit for power. The five-foot nine-inch outfielder hit 511 home runs, making him the first National Leaguer to swat over 500 homers. To do that, Ott had to be consistent, and he was. From 1928 to 1945 he led the Giants in home runs each season and led them in runs batted in (RBIs) ten times. There were two secrets to "Master Melvin's" power. The first was his ability to hit homers down the short left and right field lines in the Polo Grounds. The second was his stance. He stood on his back foot and lifted up his front foot (much like Darryl Strawberry) to increase his long-ball strength.

Willie Mays

Many regard center fielder Willie Mays as not only the finest Giant of all time, but the finest player of all time. "To watch Mays play was to watch Rembrandt paint

The San Francisco Giants Baseball Team

or [Enrico] Caruso sing," said one sportswriter.[2] Most people thought of Mays as the most exciting player of the 1950s, and his incredible catch in Game 1 of the 1954 World Series is still remembered as one of baseball's greatest plays. He won Rookie of the Year honors in 1951, was NL MVP (Most Valuable Player) in 1954, and won the Gold Glove Award every year from 1957 through 1968. Mays hit 660 homers and was elected to the Hall of Fame in 1979.

One of the most famous catches of all time: Willie Mays robs Cleveland's Vic Wertz of an extra-base hit during the 1954 World Series. Mays caught the ball 450 feet from home plate.

Juan Marichal

Juan Marichal ranks as one of the outstanding pitchers of the 1960s. In the seven-year period from 1963 to 1969, the high-kicking "Dominican Dandy" won 20 or more games six times. Over the course of his career he won 243 games while losing just 142, for a .631 won-lost percentage. Marichal won election to the Hall of Fame in 1983.

Following through on his swing, Barry Bonds watches the ball he hit leave the yard at Chicago's Wrigley Field.

The San Francisco Giants Baseball Team

Willie McCovey

Along with first baseman Orlando Cepeda, outfielder Willie McCovey was among San Francisco fans' first heroes after the Giants moved to the West Coast. Through 1999, the six-foot four-inch slugger's 521 home runs were the most by any left-handed batter in NL history. In 1959, he captured the National League Rookie of the Year Award. For the 1969 season, he hit 45 homers, drove in 126 runs, batted .320, and won NL MVP honors. "Stretch" McCovey was inducted into the Hall of Fame in 1986.

Barry Bonds

Barry Bonds may end up being the greatest Giants player of them all—even though he started his major-league career in Pittsburgh. He won two MVP Awards with the Pirates, and he added a third with the Giants in 1993. The son of former San Francisco outfielder Bobby Bonds and the godson of Willie Mays, Bonds is ranked as one of the twenty greatest position players of all time by *Total Baseball: The Official Encyclopedia of Major League Baseball*. In 1998, he became the first major-leaguer to record both 400 career stolen bases and 400 career homers.

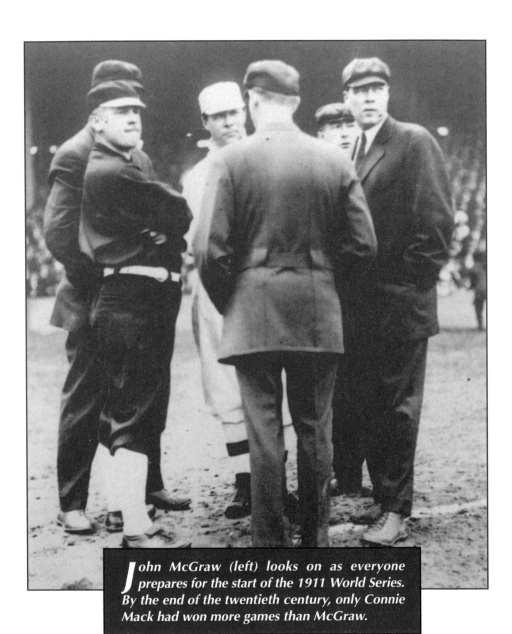

*J*ohn McGraw (left) looks on as everyone prepares for the start of the 1911 World Series. By the end of the twentieth century, only Connie Mack had won more games than McGraw.

GIANTS MANAGERS

The Giants franchise has enjoyed many outstanding managers, but only two have won election to the Baseball Hall of Fame as managers: John McGraw and Leo Durocher.

Jim Mutrie

Known for his mustache, the Giants' first noteworthy manager was "Truthful" Jim Mutrie. He gave the team its nickname, the "Giants." During one exciting game in 1885 he leapt to his feet and exclaimed, "My big fellows! My giants"—and the name stuck.[1] He won National League pennants in 1888 and 1889.

John McGraw

After Mutrie left the Giants, the New York franchise went downhill fast. But in 1902, John McGraw took over the reins of the team and turned things around. Back in the 1890s McGraw had been a star third baseman (he boasted a lifetime .334 batting average) for the Baltimore Orioles, one of the toughest teams ever assembled. The old Orioles would do anything to win—and no one ever wanted to win more than McGraw did. When McGraw became a manager, he was an even fiercer competitor—and he still knew how to win. His Giants captured pennants in 1904, 1905, 1911, 1912, 1913, 1917, 1921, 1922, 1923, and 1924. They won world championships in 1905, and in 1921 and 1922—twice defeating the rival Yankees in the World Series. "McGraw comes strutting in [saying] 'if my brains hold out, we'll win it,'" first baseman George "Highpockets" Kelly once recalled.

McGraw hated to lose, but when he did, he never looked back. In 1908, Fred Merkle made a base-running blunder that helped cost the Giants the pennant. McGraw would not let Merkle—a talented young player—get down on himself. And he even gave him a $1,000 raise.

Leo Durocher

Hall of Famers Bill Terry and Mel Ott followed McGraw as Giants manager. Terry even won three pennants, but the next great Giants manager was scrappy Leo "The Lip" Durocher. Durocher took over the Giants and transformed the team from a bunch of power-hitting also-rans into a hustling club that captured pennants in 1951 and 1954. Durocher wanted to win just as much as McGraw—maybe more. "When you're playing for money," he wrote in his autobiography, "winning is the only thing that matters.

Show me a good loser in professional sports, and I'll show you an idiot."[2]

If Durocher could not win the pennant, he lost interest in the game. "Leo could get the maximum out of you," Alvin Dark once recalled, "or get nothing. He could finish first by ten games with a fourth-place club, or last with a second place club. By July if he knew he couldn't win he could care less."[3]

Alvin Dark

Alvin Dark never had a losing season in four seasons as Giants manager. In 1962, his team won 103 games and triumphed over the Dodgers in an exciting playoff to decide the National League championship.

Frank Robinson

In 1981, the Giants hired the first African-American manager in National League history; former Reds and Orioles star Frank Robinson. "The thing about Frank is that he really hates to lose," said second baseman Joe Morgan. "And Frank makes it very uncomfortable to be around him if you do lose. A lot of people say they hate to lose, but they don't really mean it. Frank does."[4]

Roger Craig

"Slim" Craig had been a hard-luck pitcher with the early New York Mets and a successful pitching coach with Sparky Anderson's Detroit Tigers. In 1987, he led the Giants to an NL West Division title with a 90–72 mark. For the 1989 season, he took the Giants to an NL

*S*hown here during his playing days with the Baltimore Orioles, Frank Robinson became the first African American to manage in the National League.

pennant, but in that year's World Series, the team was humiliated by their cross-bay rivals, the Oakland Athletics.

Dusty Baker

In 1993, Baker's first year as Giants manager, his club won 103 games but could finish only second to the

*D*usty Baker took over as the Giants manager in 1993, winning NL manager of the year awards in 1993 and 1997.

powerful Atlanta Braves. In 1997, his team captured the NL West Division title. During the 1998 season, the Giants came from behind to tie the Cubs for the NL wild-card slot. Unfortunately, they lost out for postseason honors in a one-game playoff.

*C*andlestick Park, later renamed 3Com Park, opened as the new home of the Giants in 1960. Famous for the swirling winds, the team played its final game at 3Com in 1999.

THE CITY BY THE BAY

n 1958, the Giants arrived in San Francisco. Along with the Dodgers, they became the first teams in Major League Baseball to play on the West Coast.

A New Home

At first the Giants played at Seals Stadium, a twenty-three-thousand-seat ballpark that had served as home to the minor-league Pacific Coast League San Francisco Seals. But Seals Stadium was too small to support a major-league team, so the Giants soon made plans to move to the new Candlestick Park. Candlestick Park was much larger, and more modern, but it suffered from a huge problem—chilling, gusting winds that swirled around the park and made it uncomfortable for both Giants players and fans. During the 1961 All-Star Game held at Candlestick, pitcher Stu Miller was even blown off the pitcher's mound.

The new San Francisco version of the Giants boasted superstar Willie Mays on its roster but also featured such promising young players as first baseman Orlando Cepeda, outfielder Willie McCovey, pitcher Juan Marichal, third baseman Jim Davenport, and the three Alou brothers—Felipe, Matty, and Jesus.

1962 Playoffs

The 1962 season was nearly a replay of the exciting 1951 season. In 1962, the Los Angeles Dodgers (featuring such stars as Hall of Fame pitchers Sandy Koufax and Don Drysdale and NL Most Valuable Player Maury Wills) led the league for most of the season, but lost ten of their last thirteen games. A Los Angeles loss and a San Francisco win on the last day of the season threw the race into a tie. Once again, the two teams staged a three-game playoff, with the Giants winning the first game and losing the second.

Before 45,693 fans at Dodger Stadium, the Giants and Dodgers faced off in Game 3, with Juan Marichal starting against Dodgers southpaw Johnny Podres. The Giants jumped off to a quick 2–0 lead. In the sixth inning they loaded the bases with no one out—but failed to score. Meanwhile the Dodgers were battling back. By the eighth inning Los Angeles held a 4–2 lead. Things looked grim for the Giants in the ninth, but pinch hitter Matty Alou led off with a single. Left fielder Harvey Kuenn made an out, but then relief pitcher Ed Roebuck walked both Willie McCovey and Felipe Alou to load the bases.

The San Francisco Giants Baseball Team

*J*uan Marichal pitched for San Francisco from 1960 to 1973. He won more than twenty games in a season six times.

The Say Hey Kid and Cepeda Come Through

Willie Mays then lined a single to right, scoring Matty Alou and making it a 4–3 game. That forced Roebuck out of the game. Into the game to pitch came Stan Williams, who had won the game for the Dodgers the day before. The Giants' Orlando Cepeda then came through with a sacrifice fly to short right field that was still deep enough to score Alou with the tying run. Up came catcher Ed Bailey—and Williams launched a wild pitch that moved runners to second and third. With first base open, Williams now intentionally walked Bailey, once again loading the bases.

*D*espite playing in only ninety games in 1962, Willie McCovey hit 20 home runs for the Giants. He led the league in home runs three times during his career.

Now Jim Davenport came to the plate for San Francisco. Williams knew Davenport hit him well. So he nibbled on the corners, and his first two pitches just missed, and he was behind 2–0. He came in for a strike, but then missed again for ball three. Now he had to throw a strike.

The Giants Take the Lead

But he did not. Ball four—and the go-ahead run walked home. One more run came in when Dodgers second baseman Larry Burright booted shortstop Jose Pagan's grounder. The Giants now led 6–4, and unlike the Los Angeles bullpen that had just given up the lead, Billy Pierce made San Francisco's lead stand up in the bottom of the inning. The Giants were NL champs. A reporter wanted to know if the players were excited. "Are you crazy?" Willie Mays responded. "That was $15,000 a man!"[1]—the amount each player would receive for going to the World Series.

It was not quite as dramatic as in 1951—nothing could be after all—but it was close.

*G*iants first baseman Will Clark leaps into the air after the final out of the the 1989 NLCS. The Giants defeated the Chicago Cubs in five games to reach the World Series.

UPS AND DOWNS

The Giants won NL West titles in 1971, when they lost to the Pirates in the National League Championship Series (NLCS), and 1987, when they lost to the Cardinals. They would not win another pennant until 1989, when manager Roger Craig guided his team to a 92–70 record and a first-place finish in its division as the Giants topped the 2 million mark in attendance for the first time.

A Special Season

"People thought we couldn't win," said Craig. "They predicted we'd finish fourth or fifth, but I had the feeling the season could be special."[1] MVP outfielder Kevin Mitchell (47 HR, 125 RBIs, .291) and first baseman Will Clark (23 HR, 111 RBIs, .333) led the offense. In the NLCS, the Giants defeated the Cubs in five games. But the World Series against the Giants' local rival, the Oakland Athletics, was a complete disaster. The earthquake that rocked Game 3 was bad enough, but the Giants' performance in the Series was almost as bad—swept in four games by the combined score of 32–14.

Craig never again won with the Giants and retired after the 1992 season. Former major-league outfielder Dusty Baker replaced him and led San Francisco to a remarkable 103–59 season. Baker was not the only addition to the team. In the off-season the club had signed free agent outfielder Barry Bonds. Bonds hit .336 with 46 HR and 123 RBIs. Third baseman Matt Williams slugged 38 HR with 110 RBIs. John Burkett (22–7), Bill Swift (21–8), and Rod Beck (48 saves) led the pitching staff.

Yet the season was a disappointment. On the last day of the season, the Giants lost to the Dodgers, finishing a game behind the Atlanta Braves.

The Giants Rebuild

The Giants stumbled along for the next few seasons, finishing last (67–77) in the strike-shortened 1995 season, and again (68–94) in 1996. In 1997, however, the club turned it all around. Two huge midseason trades helped. In one, Matt Williams went to Cleveland in exchange for second baseman Jeff Kent and shortstop Jose Vizcaino. The second trade brought in pitchers Wilson Alvarez, Roberto Hernandez, and Danny Darwin from the Chicago White Sox. The team finished 90–72, first in the NL West. "This team is defined by emotion," said general manager Brian Sabean, "and emotion is spontaneous."[2] In the NL

*M*att Williams was the Giants third baseman from 1987 to 1996. Williams won three Gold Glove awards with San Francisco, and was selected to play in four All-Star Games.

*J*eff Kent led all major-league second basemen in RBIs in 1998, helping guide the Giants to a one-game playoff to decide the National League's wild-card spot.

Division playoffs, however, the Giants were swept by the NL's wild-card team, and eventual World Series champion, the Florida Marlins.

The Giants played sluggishly through most of 1998, and were five games behind in the loss column with just ten days to play. They seemed out of not only the division race but also the NL wild-card chase. They then won nine of eleven games to move ahead of the New York Mets and force a tie with the Chicago Cubs. On the last day of the season, they took a 7–0 lead against the Colorado Rockies—and seemed on the verge of winning it all—but blew the lead and lost 9–8.

One-Game Playoff

Their loss forced a one-game playoff with the Cubs, which San Francisco lost, 5–3. Still, some Giants enjoyed an impressive season in 1998. Jeff Kent hit 31 homers and drove in 128 runs. Barry Bonds became the first player with 400 career homers and 400 career steals, as he hit .303 with 37 homers, 122 RBIs, and 28 stolen bases.

In 1999, the Giants finished second to the surprising Arizona Diamondbacks. During the season, *The Sporting News* named Bonds as its Player of the Decade.

At the turn of the new century, the Giants opened a brand new ballpark. Pacific Bell Park is located in the city of San Francisco's China Basin neighborhood. Costing $262 million, the park can seat forty-two thousand fans. It is a great park for a great team.

STATISTICS

Team Record

The Giants History

YEARS	LOCATION	W	L	PCT.	PENNANTS	WORLD CHAMPION
1883–89	New York	503	316	.614	1888–89	None*
1890–99	New York	711	660	.519	None	None
1900–09	New York	823	645	.561	1904–05	1905*
1910–19	New York	889	597	.598	1911–13, 1917	None
1920–29	New York	890	639	.58?	1921–24	1921–22
1930–39	New York	868	657	.569	1933, 1936–37	1933
1940–49	New York	724	808	.473	None	None
1950–59	New York San Francisco**	822	721	.533	1951, 1954	1954
1960–69	San Francisco	902	704	.562	1962	None
1970–79	San Francisco	794	818	.493	None	None
1980–89	San Francisco	773	795	.493	1989	None
1990–99	San Francisco	790	766	.508	None	None

The Giants Today

YEAR	W	L	PCT.	MANAGER	DIVISION FINISH
1990	85	77	.525	Roger Craig	3
1991	75	87	.463	Roger Craig	4
1992	72	90	.444	Roger Craig	5
1993	103	59	.636	Dusty Baker	2
1994	55	60	.478	Dusty Baker	2

The San Francisco Giants

The Giants Today (con't)

YEAR	W	L	PCT.	MANAGER	DIVISION FINISH
1995	67	77	.465	Dusty Baker	4
1996	68	94	.420	Dusty Baker	4
1997	90	72	.556	Dusty Baker	1
1998	89	74	.546	Dusty Baker	2
1999	86	76	.531	Dusty Baker	2

Total History

W	L	PCT.	PENNANTS	WORLD SERIES
9,489	8,126	.539	19	5*

W=Wins   L=Losses   PCT.=Winning Percentage
PENNANTS=Won League Title   WORLD SERIES=Won World Series.

*The Giants were the NL champions in 1888, 1889, and 1904, but did not participate in the modern World Series until the 1905 season.
**Giants moved to San Francisco prior to the 1958 season.

Championship Managers

MANAGER	YEARS MANAGED	RECORD	CHAMPIONSHIPS
James Mutrie	1885–91	529–345	National League, 1888–89
John McGraw	1902–32	2,583–1,790	World Series, 1905, 1921–22 National League, 1904, 1911–13, 1917, 1923–24
Bill Terry	1932–41	823–661	World Series, 1933 National League, 1936–37
Leo Durocher	1948–55	637–523	World Series, 1954 National League, 1951
Alvin Dark	1961–64	366–277	National League, 1962
Roger Craig	1985–92	586–566	National League, 1989
Dusty Baker	1993–	558–512	NL West Division, 1997

Great Hitters

PLAYER	SEA	YRS	G	AB	R	H	HR	RBI	SB	AVG
Barry Bonds	1993–99	14	2,000	6,976	1,455	2,010	445	1,299	460	.288
Orlando Cepeda*	1958–66	17	2,124	7,927	1,131	2,351	379	1,365	142	.297
Frankie Frisch*	1919–26	19	2,311	9,112	1,532	2,880	105	1,244	419	.316
Monte Irvin*	1949–55	8	764	2,499	366	731	99	443	28	.293
Travis Jackson*	1922–36	15	1,656	6,086	833	1,768	135	929	71	.291
Willie Mays*	1951–52 1954–72	22	2,992	10,881	2,062	3,283	660	1,903	338	.302
Willie McCovey*	1959–73 1977–80	22	2,588	8,197	1,229	2,211	521	1,555	26	.270
Mel Ott*	1926–47	22	2,730	9,456	1,859	2,876	511	1,860	89	.304
Bill Terry*	1923–36	14	1,721	6,428	1,120	2,193	154	1,078	56	.341
Bobby Thomson	1946–53 1957	15	1,779	6,305	903	1,705	264	1,026	38	.270

CAREER STATISTICS

SEA=Seasons with Giants   AB=At-bats   HR=Home Runs   SB=Stolen Bases
YRS=Years in the Majors   R=Runs Scored   RBI=Runs Batted In   AVG=Batting Average
G=Games   H=Hits   *Member of National Baseball Hall of Fame

Great Pitchers

CAREER STATISTICS

PLAYER	SEA	YRS	W	L	PCT.	ERA	G	SV	IP	K	SH
Rod Beck	1991–97	9	26	37	.413	3.20	540	260	587.1	499	0
Freddie Fitzsimmons	1925–37	19	217	146	.598	3.51	513	13	3,223.2	870	29
Carl Hubbell*	1928–43	16	253	154	.622	2.98	535	33	3,590.1	1,677	36
Juan Marichal*	1960–73	16	243	142	.631	2.89	471	2	3,507.1	2,303	52
Christy Mathewson*	1900–16	17	373	188	.665	2.13	635	28	4,780.2	2,502	79

SEA=Seasons with Giants   L=Losses   G=Games   K=Strikeouts
YRS=Years in the Majors   PCT.=Winning Percentage   SV=Saves   SH=Shutouts
W=Wins   ERA=Earned Run Average   IP=Innings Pitched
*Member of National Baseball Hall of Fame

CHAPTER NOTES

Chapter 1. "The Giants Win the Pennant"

1. Leo Durocher, with Ed Linn, *Nice Guys Finish Last* (New York: Simon & Schuster, 1975), p. 300.

2. Ray Robinson, *The Home Run Heard 'Round the World: The Dramatic Story of the 1951 Giants-Dodgers Pennant Race* (New York: HarperCollins, 1991), p. 226.

3. Damon Rice, *Seasons Past* (New York: Praeger, 1976), p. 373.

4. Curt Smith, *Voices of the Game: The First Full-Scale Overview of Baseball Broadcasting, 1921 to the Present* (South Bend, Ind.: Diamond Communications, 1987), pp. 266–267.

Chapter 2. New York, New York

1. Joe Durso, *Casey and Mr. McGraw* (St. Louis, Mo.: The Sporting News Publishing Company, 1989), p. 61.

2. Dan Schlossberg, *The New Baseball Catalog* (Middle Village, N.Y.: Jonathan David Publishers, 1998), p. 47.

Chapter 3. Giant Immortals

1. Paul Dickson, *Baseball's Greatest Quotations* (New York: HarperCollins, 1991), p. 261.

2. Kevin Nelson, *Baseball's Greatest Quotes* (New York: Simon & Schuster, 1982), p. 77.

Chapter 4. Giants Managers

1. Frank Graham, *The New York Giants* (New York: G. P. Putnam & Sons, 1952), p. 9.

2. Leo Durocher, with Ed Linn, *Nice Guys Finish Last* (New York: Simon & Schuster, 1975), p. 11.

3. Alvin Dark, with John Underwood, *When in Doubt, Fire the Manager: My Life and Times in Baseball* (New York: Dutton, 1980), pp. 58–59.

4. Frank Robinson and Berry Stainback, *Extra Innings* (New York: McGraw Hill, 1988), p. 175.

Chapter 5. The City by the Bay

1. David Plaut, *Chasing October: The Dodgers-Giants Pennant Race of 1962* (South Bend, Ind.: Diamond Communications, 1994), p. 186.

Chapter 6. Ups and Downs

1. Paul White, ed., *USA Today Baseball Weekly 1998 Almanac* (New York: Henry Holt, 1998), p. 275.

2. John Shea and John Hickey, *Magic by the Bay* (Berkeley, Calif.: North Atlantic Books, 1990), p. vii.

GLOSSARY

American Association—A defunct major league that operated from 1882 to 1891. Not to be confused with a later minor league by the same name.

American League—One of the two current major leagues of baseball, founded in 1901 by Ban Johnson. The other major league is the National League. The primary difference between the two leagues is that since 1973 the American League (AL) has used the designated hitter rule.

batting average—Number of hits divided by times at-bat.

Cooperstown—A small town in Upstate New York that is the home of the National Baseball Hall of Fame. At one time it was believed baseball was invented in Cooperstown.

Cy Young Award—Award given each year to the best pitcher in each major league.

designated hitter—A player who does not take the field during the game, but only bats. In the major leagues, the designated hitter (DH) is used only in American League ballparks.

ERA (Earned Run Average)—The number of earned runs allowed, divided by the number of innings pitched, times nine; the ERA is perhaps the best measure of pitching effectiveness.

free agent—A major-leaguer whose contractual obligations to his old team have expired and who is free to sign with any major-league team.

general manager—The official in charge of a ballclub's business and personnel matters.

Gold Glove Award—Award given annually to the best fielder at each position in both the National and American Leagues.

Hall of Fame—Located in Cooperstown, N.Y., membership in the National Baseball Hall of Fame is the highest honor that can be awarded to a professional player.

homer—Home run.

infielder—One who plays an infield position (first, second, or third base or shortstop).

League Championship Series—The best-of-seven series that determines the American and National League champions.

MVP Award—Most Valuable Player Award; voted on by members of the Baseball Writers Association of America (BBWAA).

National League—The oldest surviving major league, founded in 1876 by William Hulbert, sometimes called the "senior circuit."

pennant—A league championship, alternately called the "flag."

RBI—Run(s) batted in.

rookie—A first-year player.

Rookie of the Year Award—Award given each year to an outstanding rookie in each major league. It was first awarded in 1947 to the Brooklyn Dodgers' Jackie Robinson.

screwball—A pitch that breaks the opposite direction of a curve. A screwball thrown by a left-hander will break away from a right-handed batter.

southpaw—A left-handed pitcher.

stolen base—A play in which the base runner advances to another base while the pitcher is in his motion, and without the pitch being batted.

umpire—The official in baseball who makes the necessary decisions (such as safe or out, balls or strikes, fair or foul) during a game.

wild-card—The nondivision winning club with the best won-lost percentage in regular-season play; the wild-card team in each league earns a berth in postseason play.

World Series—The end of the season best-of-seven series that pits the champions of the National and American Leagues against each other.

FURTHER READING

Bitker, Steve. *The Original San Francisco Giants: The Giants of '58.* Champaign, Ill.: Sagamore, 1998.

Cepeda, Orlando, and Herb Fagen. *Baby Bull; From Hardball to Hard Time and Back.* Dallas: Taylor, 1998.

Dickey, Glenn. *San Francisco Giants: 40 Years.* San Francisco: Woodford Publishing, 1997.

Durocher, Leo, with John Underwood. *Nice Guys Finish Last.* New York: Simon & Schuster, 1975.

Gershman, Michael. *Diamonds: The Evolution of the Ballpark.* Boston: Houghton Mifflin, 1993.

Kiernan, Thomas. *The Miracle at Coogan's Bluff.* New York: Thomas Y. Crowell, 1975.

Mays, Willie, with Len Sahadi. *Say Hey: The Autobiography of Willie Mays.* New York: Simon & Schuster, 1988.

McGraw, John J. *My Thirty Years in Baseball.* Lincoln, Nebr.: University of Nebraska Press, 1995.

Muskat, Carrie. *Barry Bonds.* Broomall, Pa.: Chelsea House, 1997.

Pietrusza, David. *Top 10 Baseball Managers.* Springfield, N.J.: Enslow Publishers Inc., 1998.

Plaut, David. *Chasing October: The Dodgers-Giants Pennant Race of 1962.* South Bend, Ind.: Diamond Communications, 1994.

Shea, John, and John Hickey. *Magic by the Bay: How the Oakland Athletics and San Francisco Giants Captured the Baseball World.* Berkeley, Calif.: North Atlantic Books, 1990.

Sullivan, Michael J. *Sports Great Barry Bonds.* Springfield, N.J.: Enslow Publishers, Inc., 1995.

Thomson, Bobby, with Lee Heiman and Bill Gutman. *The Giants Win the Pennant! The Giants Win the Pennant!* New York: Kensington, 1991.

Thorn, John, Pete Palmer, Michael Gershman, and David Pietrusza, eds. *Total Baseball.* 6th ed. New York: Total Sports, 1999.

Williams, Peter. *When the Giants Were the Giants: Bill Terry and the Golden Age of New York Baseball.* Chapel Hill, N.C.: Algonquin, 1994.

The San Francisco Giants Baseball Team

INDEX

A

Alou, Felipe, 30
Alou, Jesus, 30
Alou, Matty, 30, 32
Alvarez, Wilson, 36
Anderson, Sparky, 25
Arizona Diamondbacks, 39
Atlanta Braves, 27, 36

B

Bailey, Ed, 32
Baker, Dusty, 26–27, 36
Baltimore Orioles (1901–02), 11, 24
Baltimore Orioles (1954–), 25
Beck, Rod, 36, 42
Bonds, Barry, 17, 21, 36, 39
Boston Red Sox, 12
Branca, Ralph, 6, 7
Bresnahan, Roger, 11
Brooklyn Dodgers, 5–7, 15
Burkett, John, 36
Burright, Larry, 33

C

Campanella, Roy, 5
Candlestick Park, 29
Cepeda, Orlando, 21, 30
Chicago Cubs, 12, 27, 35, 39
Chicago White Sox, 36
Cincinnati Reds, 25
Cleveland Indians, 15, 36
Colorado Rockies, 39
Craig, Roger "Slim," 25, 35, 36

D

Dark, Alvin, 5, 15, 25
Darwin, Danny, 36
Davenport, Jim, 30, 33
Detroit Tigers, 25
Drysdale, Don, 30
Durocher, Leo, 5, 6, 7, 9, 15, 23, 24–25

F

Freedman, Andrew, 11
Frisch, Frankie, 12

H

Hartung, Clint, 7
Hernandez, Roberto, 36
Hodges, Gil, 6
Hodges, Russ, 7, 9
Hubbell, "King Carl," 13

I

Irvin, Monte, 5, 6, 7, 15

J

Jackson, Travis "Stonewall," 12–13
Jansen, Larry, 5, 6

K

Kelly, George "Highpockets," 12, 24
Kent, Jeff, 36, 38, 39
Koufax, Sandy, 30
Kuenn, Johnny, 30

L

Lindstrom, Fred, 12
Lockman, Whitey, 7
Los Angeles Dodgers, 15, 25, 29, 30, 31, 32, 33, 36

M

Mack, Connie, 17–18, 22
Maglie, Sal, 5
Marichal, Juan, 20, 30
Mathewson, Christy, 11–12, 17–18
Mays, Willie, 5, 15, 18–19, 21, 30, 32, 33
McCovey, Willie, 21, 30
McGinnity, Joe "Iron Man," 11
McGraw, John, 11, 12, 13, 18, 23–24
Merkle, Fred, 12, 24
Miller, Stu, 29
Mitchell, Kevin, 35
Morgan, Joe, 25

Mueller, Don, 6, 7
Mutrie, Jim, 11, 23

N

New York Mets, 25, 39
New York Yankees, 13, 24
Newcombe, Don, 7

O

Oakland Athletics, 26, 35
Ott, Mel, 13, 15, 18, 24

P

Pacific Bell Park, 39
Pagan, Jose, 33
Philadelphia A's, 12, 17
Pierce, Billy, 33
Pittsburgh Pirates, 21, 35
Podres, Johnny, 30
Polo Grounds, 18

R

Reese, Pee Wee, 5
Robinson, Frank, 25
Robinson, Jackie, 5
Roebuck, Ed, 30, 32

Ruth, Babe, 13

S

Sabean, Brian, 36
St. Louis Cardinals, 35
Seals Stadium, 29
Snider, Duke, 5
Snodgrass, Fred, 12
Stanky, Eddie "The Brat," 15
Strawberry, Darryl, 18
Swift, Bill, 36

T

Terry, Bill, 13, 15, 18, 24
Thomson, Bobby, 5, 6, 7, 9, 15
Troy Trojans, 11

V

Vizcaino, Jose, 36

W

Washington Senators, 18
Williams, Matt, 36
Williams, Stan, 32, 33

Y

Youngs, Ross "Pep," 13

WHERE TO WRITE

San Francisco Giants
Pacific Bell Park
24 Willie Mays Plaza
San Francisco, CA
94124-2618

WEB SITES

http://www.sfgiants.com
http://www.majorleaguebaseball.com/nl/sf